W9-CFX-900

JESUS GOES TO THE SYNAGOGUE

A story of what might have happened one day when Jesus was a child.

HELEN BROWN

Illustrated by Nell Fisher

ISBN 0-687-09035-0

TEXT COPYRIGHT © 1963 BY ABINGDON PRESS. ART COPYRIGHT © 1999 BY ABINGDON PRESS.
ALL RIGHTS RESERVED.

ABINGDON PRESS
MANUFACTURED IN HONG KONG

99 00 01 02 03 04 05 06 07 08 – 10 9 8 7 6 5 4 3 2 1

It was the Sabbath day.

It was time to go to the synagogue.

Jesus and Joseph started up the hill.

Close behind were Jesus' mother, Mary;

his baby sister; and his brothers,

James, Joses, and Simon.

Jesus was excited. He was just thirteen. And now for the first time he could sit with the men at the regular synagogue service. He could hardly wait to get to the synagogue.

The synagogue in Nazareth, like every

synagogue, was built on the highest place in the

village. It was a long, hard climb from Jesus'

house. Halfway up the hill little Joses and

Simon had to rest.

While they stopped, Jesus put on his cap

and prayer shawl. All men and boys had to have

their heads covered in the synagogue.

When they got to the top of the hill, the family went into the synagogue together.

Joseph put the family's offering into the box that stood by the door.

Mary, baby sister, James, Joses, and Simon went up the stairs to the gallery.

Always before, Jesus had gone up the stairs, too.

Always before, Jesus had sat with his mother.

But on this Sabbath day, Joseph took Jesus gently by the arm.

Together they poured water over their hands to wash them.

Together they walked to seats

along the wall.

Together they sat down near the three

men who were to be the readers for the day.

Beside the readers stood Nathan, Rabbi Ezra's helper. He was counting the men and older boys as they entered the synagogue.

When Jesus and Joseph came in, there were ten. When ten men were there, the synagogue service could begin. So now the service could start.

Rabbi Ezra stood up.

Slowly he raised his arms.

"Hear, O Israel; the Lord our God is one Lord," he said.

Then he and the people repeated together the rest of the Shema.

"**Y**ou shall love the Lord your God with all your heart and with all your soul and with all your might."

Next came the prayers.

Rabbi Ezra turned around. With his back to the people, he prayed.

And then several other men prayed.

After each prayer, Jesus, Joseph, and all the rest of the people said, "Amen."

When the prayers were over, Rabbi Ezra's helper, Nathan, went to the tall cupboard where the scrolls were kept. The cupboard was called *the Ark.*

Nathan drew back the curtains of the Ark and took out one scroll. He carried it to the reader's desk.

The scroll was wrapped in a beautiful silk cover. Jesus could see it very clearly.

One of the readers got up and took off the cover.

Then everyone began to chant, "The earth is full of the steadfast love of the Lord."

The reader read some verses, and the people chanted others. Jesus was glad that he knew the Psalms and could join the others in thanking God.

When the reading was over, Nathan returned the first scroll to the Ark and took the Scroll of the Law to the reader's desk.

After removing the cover, the second reader held the scroll high over his head.

Everyone said, "This is the law. . . . 'The law of the Lord is perfect.'"

Jesus listened hard to the laws as the reader read them.

The third reader read from the Scroll of the Prophets. He read about the prophet called Micah.

While Jesus listened, he thought, *I must always remember "to do justice and to love kindness" as Micah said.*

When the third scroll was put

back in the Ark, Rabbi Ezra talked about Micah.

The rabbi answered some questions about

the prophet and his teachings.

Finally Rabbi Ezra slowly raised his arms again.

Everyone chanted, "I was glad when they said to me, 'Let us go to the house of the Lord!'"

Jesus felt very glad to be there.

Then Rabbi Ezra stood with his back to the people.

"The Lord bless you and keep you," he prayed.

Jesus, his father, and all the others added, "Amen."

Jesus left the synagogue

with Joseph.

When Mary joined them,

she said, "It is a happy day for

all of us. I am glad that

you are old enough

to sit with the

men in the

synagogue."

Jesus smiled.
He was happy, too.

Jesus would always remember this synagogue service and this Sabbath day.